Ocean Life

Sally Morgan
Activities by Tracey E. Dils

Sandy Creek

Authors Tracey E. Dils and Sally Morgan
Consultant Camilla de la Bédoyère
Editors Sarah Eason and Eve Marleau
Designers Calcium and Lisa Peacock
Picture Researcher Maria Joannou
Illustrator Mike Byrne and Geoff Ward

Associate Publisher Zeta Davies
Editorial Director Jane Walker

Sandy Creek
122 Fifth Avenue
New York, NY 10011

ISBN 978 1 4351 2336 6

A CIP record for this book is available from the Library of Congress.

10 9 8 7 6 5 4 3 2 1

Printed and bound in China

Picture credits
Key: t = top, b = bottom, c = center,
l = left, r = right, FC = front cover,
BC = back cover

FC: Shutterstock; 1: t Denis Scott/ Corbis, l Shutterstock, c Shutterstock, r Dreamstime; 2: Dreamstime; 5: l Science Faction/Getty, r Oxford Scientific/Photo Library; 7: all images Shutterstock; 8-9: Bruce Rasner/Rotman/Naturepi; 8: b Toru Yamanaka/AFP/Getty; 11: Bruce Rasner/Rotman/Naturepi; 12-13: Earth Scenes/Animals Animals/Photo Library; 12: b Dreamstime; 13: t Brian J Skerry/ National Geographic/Getty; 15: all images Shutterstock; 16-17: Darlyne A Murawski/ National Geographic/Getty; 16: b Peter David/Taxi/Getty; 17: r Norbert Wu/ Minden Pictures/Getty; 17: Norbert Wu/ Minden Pictures/Getty; 20-21: Norbert Wu/Minden Pictures/Getty; 20: b Norbert Wu/Minden Pictures/FLPA; 22: c Peter David/Taxi/Getty, all other images Shutterstock; 21: Norbert Wu/ Minden Pictures/Getty; 24-25: Jim Watt/ Pacific Stock/Photo Library; 24: cb Oxford Scientific/Photo Library; 25: all images Shutterstock; 28-29: Shutterstock; 28: l Shutterstock, r Shutterstock; 29: r Harold Taylor/Photolibrary; 32-33: Brandon Cole /Corbis; 33: b Theo Allofs/ Corbis, t Istockphoto; 36-37: Duncan Murrell/ Photo Library; 36: b Paul A Souders/ Corbis, t James Watt/Photo Library; 38: all images Shutterstock; 40-41: James Watt/Photo Library; 40: b Istockphoto; 41: t Istockphoto; 44-45: Rodger Jackman/ Photo Library; 44: l Istockphoto; 45: b Amos Nachoum/ Corbis; 46: all images Shutterstock; 48: l Dreamstime, r Dreamstime; 49: br Dreamstime, t Dreamstime; 52-53: James Watt/Photo Library; 53: b Stuart Westmorland/Corbis; 54: t Dreamstime, b Shutterstock; 56-57: Shutterstock; 56: l Istockphoto; 57: r David Nardini; 60-61: Shutterstock; 60: l Dreamstime; 61: r Dreamstime; 62: all images Shutterstock, 64-65: Mauritius Die Bildagentur Gmbh/ Photo Library; 64: l Dreamstime; 65: t Shutterstock, r Nic Bothma/epa/Corbis; 66: all images Shutterstock; 68-69: Shutterstock; 64: b Shutterstock; 70: all images Shutterstock; 71: all images Shutterstock; 72-73: Shutterstock; 72: b Shutterstock; 73: t Shutterstock; 75: all images Shutterstock; 76-77: Shutterstock; 76: b Kevin Schafer/ Corbis; 77: t Andy Rouse/Corbis; 78: all images Shutterstock; 80-81: Robert Yin/ Corbis; 80: l Dreamstime; 81: b Georgette Douwma/ Science Photo Library; 82: all images Shutterstock; 84-85: Shutterstock; 84: b Ralph A Clevenger/Flint Collection/ Photo Library; 85: r Shutterstock; 88-89: Shutterstock; 88: b Reinhard Dirscherl/ Mauritius/Photo Library; 89: t Anthony Bannister/Animals Animals/Photo Library; 90: all images Shutterstock; 92-93: Niall Benvie/Oxford Scientific/Photo Library; 92: b B Borrell Casals/Frank Lane Picture Agency/Corbis; 95: tl Osben, all other images Shutterstock; 96-97: Shutterstock; 96: l Reinhard Dirscherl/Ecoscene; 97: r Lawson Wood/Corbis; 98-99: all images Shutterstock; 100-101: David B Fleetham/ Pacific Stock/Photo Library; 100: l Shutterstock; 101: l David B Fleetham/ Pacific Stock/Photo Library; 104-105: Shutterstock; 104: b Tom Brakefield/Corbis; 105: r David B Fleetham/Pacific Stock/ Photo Library; 107: Shutterstock; 108-109: FI Online/Photo Library; 108: l Reinhard Dirscherl/Ecoscene; 110: Shutterstock; 111: Shutterstock; 112-113: Shutterstock; 112: b Istockphoto; 113: t Istockphoto; 114: Shutterstock; 115: all images Shutterstock.

WARNiNG
Where you see this symbol, ask an adult for help.

Words in **bold** can be found in the glossary on page 116.

Contents

Deep ocean

People splash and swim on the surface of the ocean, but its waters spread thousands of miles below. In these dark depths are huge underwater mountains and giant valleys.

Scientists explore the deep ocean in special submersibles that take them down to the seabed.

Plenty of light

Surface zone: 0–650 ft (0–200 m)

Twilight zone: 650–3,300 ft (200–1,000 m)

A little light

No light

Dark zone: 3,300–16,500 ft (1,000–5,000 m)

Valley

There are many different layers in the ocean.

Apart from the surface layer, ocean water is icy cold and dark. The animals that live here have found ways of surviving in this difficult environment.

So far, scientists have explored only a small area of the deep ocean, and they are discovering strange new animals all the time.

The hatchet fish is one of the many strange fish that live in the deep.

SINK OR SWIM

You will need:
- Bucket, sink, or bathtub
- Coin
- Nail
- Orange (unpeeled)
- Paper clip
- Pencil
- Ruler
- Rubber ball
- Water

The deep, deep sea

Which objects float and which objects sink? Find out with this fun experiment about weight and water.

WOW!
There are more than 28,000 different kinds of fish in the world's oceans.

1. Fill the bucket, sink, or bathtub with tap water.

2. Take each object and put it in the water.

3. Write what you find here. Put an "X" to show whether each object floated or sank.

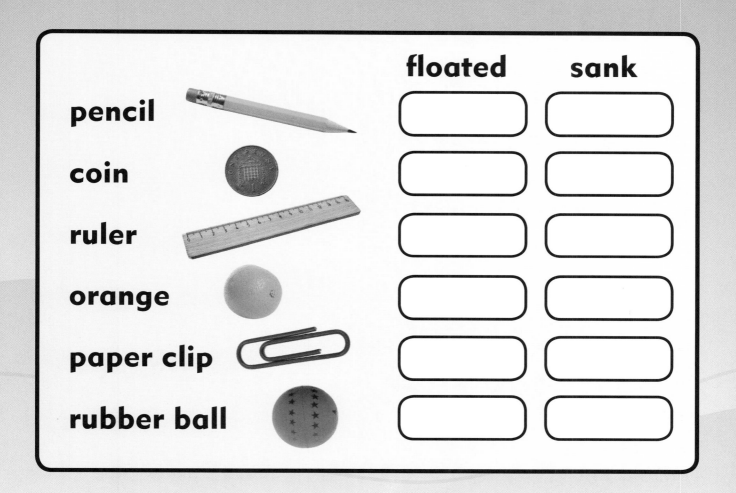

	floated	sank
pencil		
coin		
ruler		
orange		
paper clip		
rubber ball		

What happened?

The items that floated weigh less than the water. We say they are less dense. The items that sank weigh more than the water. We say they are more dense.

Megamouth sharks

This shark was first discovered in 1976. Since then, only about 40 have been seen. It lives in deep water, where it is dark and very cold.

The megamouth shark is so called because of its huge mouth and rubbery lips. It swims slowly with its mouth wide open. This lets the shark take in massive amounts of water to trap prey, such as **shrimp**, in its **gills**.

The megamouth shark's mouth is so large, it could swallow small children.

Unlike other sharks, which have **muscular** bodies, the megamouth shark has a flabby body. It does not need to swim quickly to catch fish, which is why its muscles are weaker than those of most other sharks.

The megamouth shark has a large head. Its body grows to about 16 feet (5.3 meters) long—about as long as a car.

Word up

Trace the letters that spell "shark."
Try and write the word yourself on
the writing line below.

WOW!
The biggest
megamouth shark ever
seen was 16 feet
(5.3 meters) long!

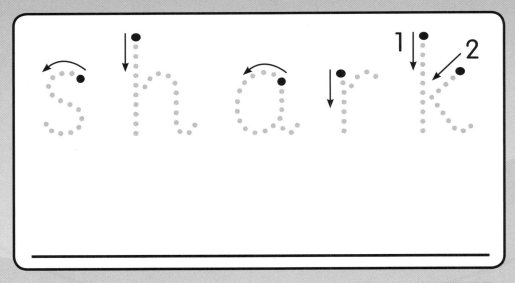

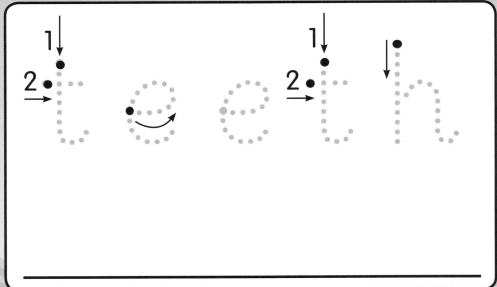

Mixed-up megamouth

Draw a line from the scrambled version of the word about megamouth sharks to the correctly spelled word.

fabbly	**mouth**
outhm	**shrimp**
shrpim	**gills**
llgis	**flabby**
usmcels	**swallow**
swalowl	**muscles**

Giant squid

Giant squid can grow to about 40 feet (13 meters) long and weigh as much as one ton—that's as long as a bus and as heavy as a car!

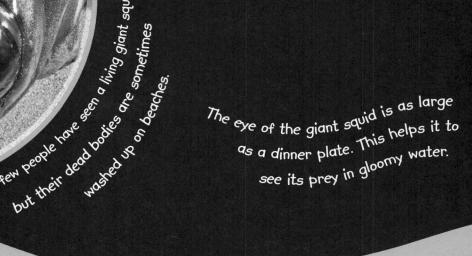

Only a few people have seen a living giant squid, but their dead bodies are sometimes washed up on beaches.

The eye of the giant squid is as large as a dinner plate. This helps it to see its prey in gloomy water.

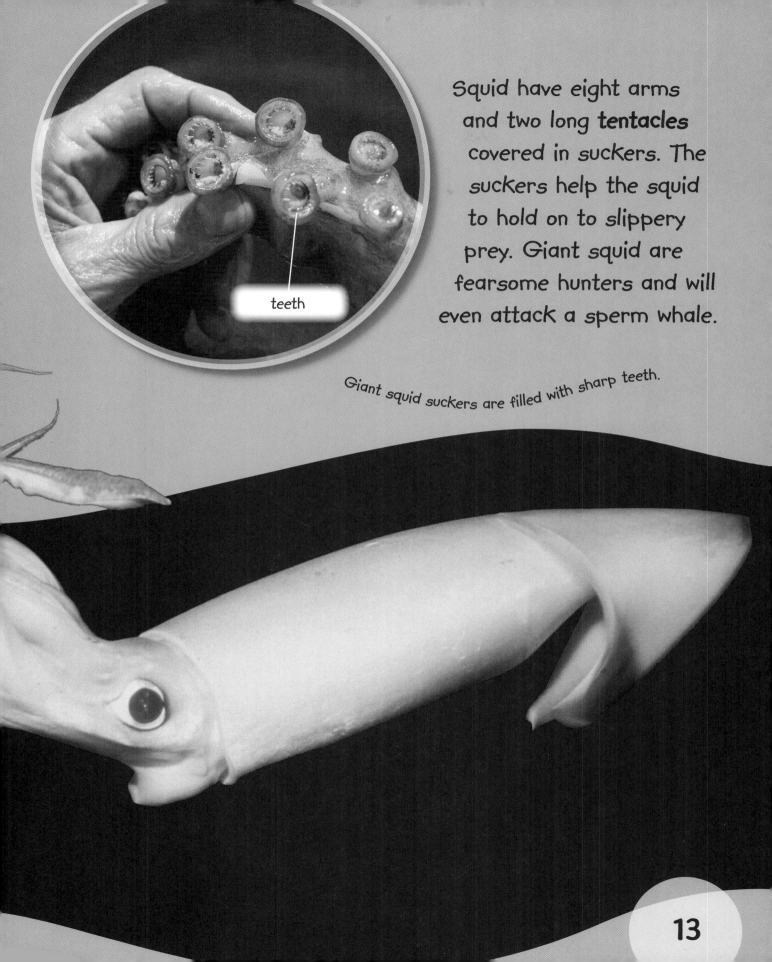

teeth

Squid have eight arms and two long **tentacles** covered in suckers. The suckers help the squid to hold on to slippery prey. Giant squid are fearsome hunters and will even attack a sperm whale.

Giant squid suckers are filled with sharp teeth.

How many arms?

Squid have eight arms. Circle the squid that have the wrong number of arms, then color the ones that have the correct number of arms.

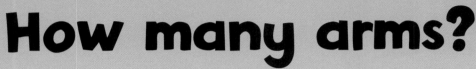

How big?

A giant squid can weigh up to one ton. Color the item that weighs as much as a giant squid. Look at page 12 for a clue.

Eye-to-eye

A giant squid's eye can be as big as one of the items below. Circle the one that is correct. Look at page 12 for a clue!

Angler fish

The angler fish lives in the darkest depths of the ocean. It has a long spine, which dangles from the top of its head. At the end of the spine is a light. The angler fish uses the light to attract its prey. The light is made by tiny creatures called bacteria, which live at the end of the spine.

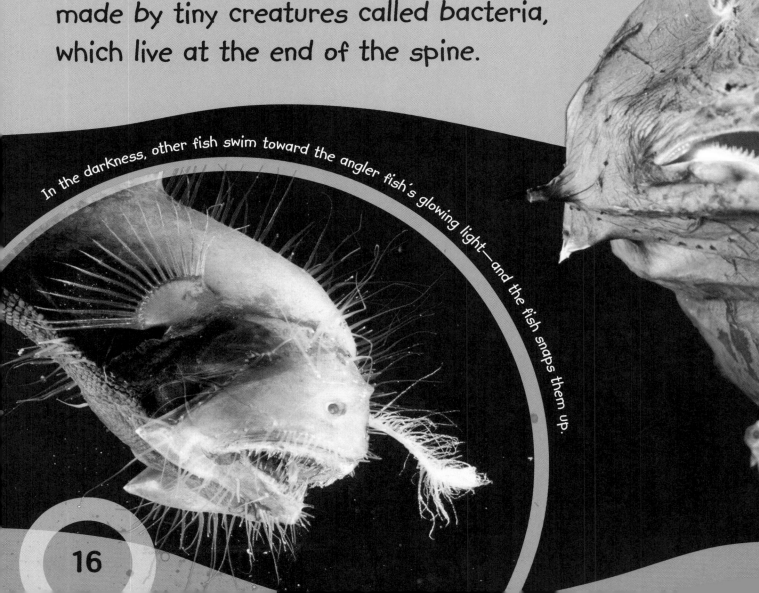

In the darkness, other fish swim toward the angler fish's glowing light—and the fish snaps them up.

The angler fish has a huge head and a very wide mouth.

Angler fish can open their jaws wide to swallow fish as large as themselves.

Angler fish have long, dagger-like teeth that point backward. They use their teeth to catch passing prey.

Angler fish mania

Practice writing these words that have to do with an angler fish. Trace them first, then write them on the lines.

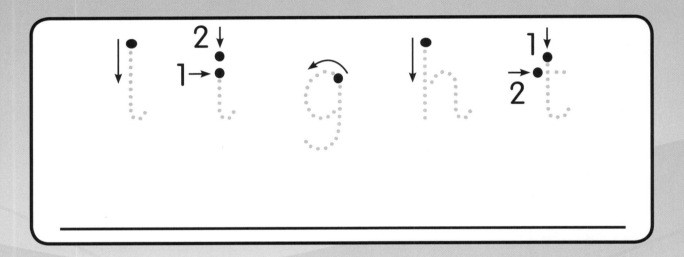

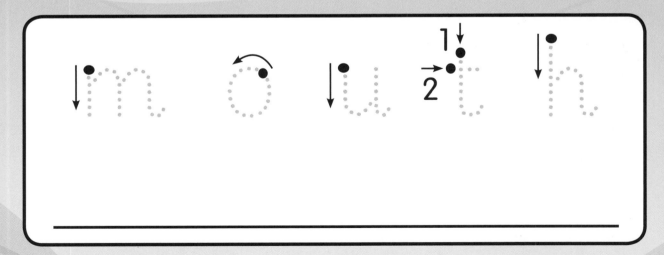

Light the way!

Complete the sentences below by matching them with the words in the word bank. Take a look at pages 16 and 17 for some clues!

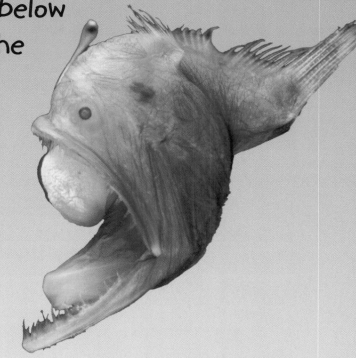

light	spine
teeth	mouth

An angler fish has a long _____ .

An angler fish has a _____ on its spine.

An angler fish has a wide _____ .

An angler fish has sharp _____ .

Viperfish and gulper eels

It is hard to find food in the ocean's deepest zone. Viperfish and gulper eels lurk in the waters, waiting for prey to pass or a dead creature to sink from the surface waters.

The gulper eel has a hinged mouth, which can open wide to swallow prey larger than itself.

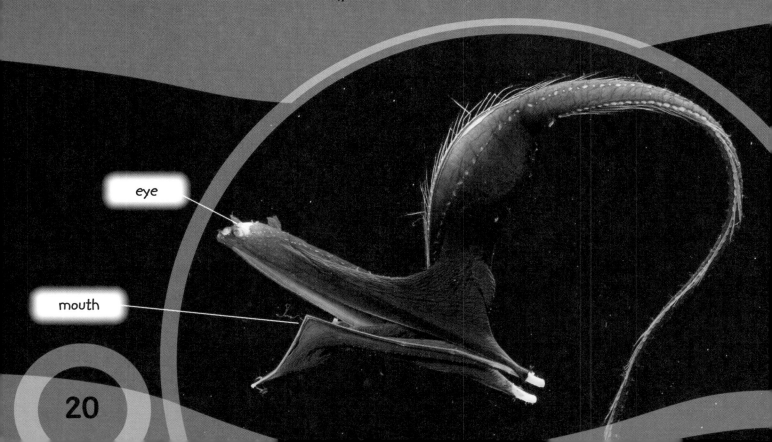

eye

mouth

Viperfish and gulper eels have knife-like teeth that grip prey so it cannot escape. Their huge stomach stretches so they can gobble up passing prey of any size.

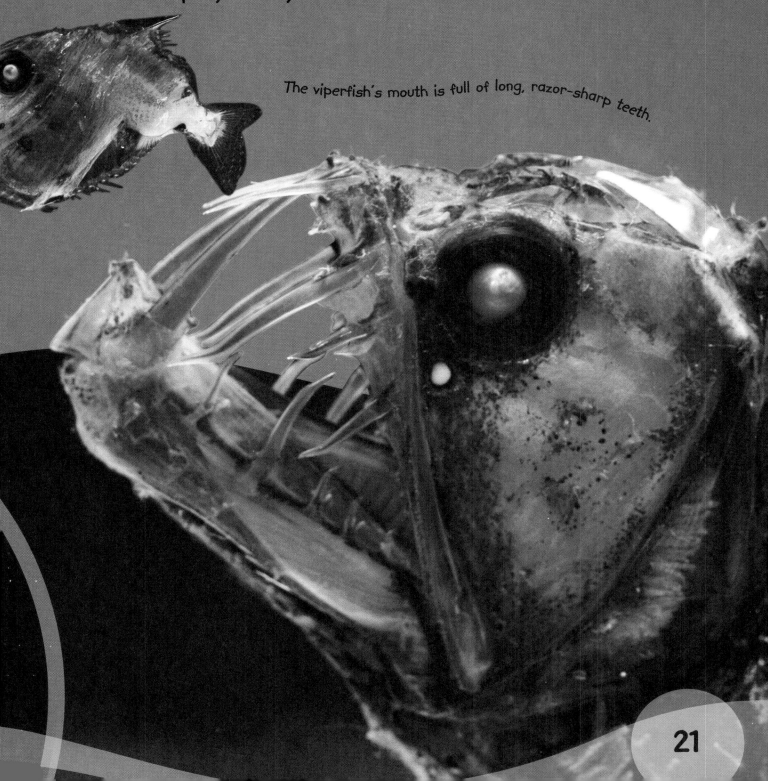

The viperfish's mouth is full of long, razor-sharp teeth.

What's for dinner?

Count how many of each kind of prey there are in the ocean for the gulper eel to eat. Write the answers in the boxes below.

shrimp ☐ crab ☐ fish ☐

How long?

Viperfish are small but fierce. Measure the viperfish below and write how many inches each fish is in the boxes.

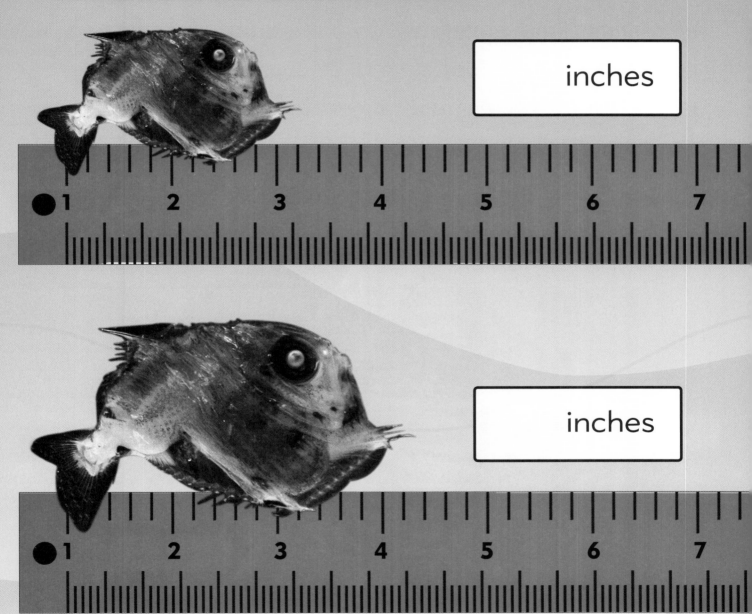

inches

inches

Nautiluses

The nautilus has lived in the world's deep oceans for millions of years. It is a type of mollusc and is related to the squid. It is called a head-foot animal because its feet (the tentacles) are joined to its head.

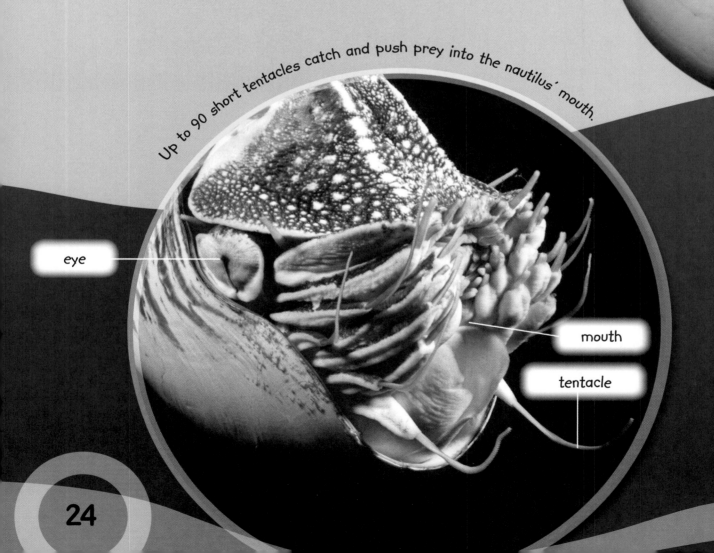

Up to 90 short tentacles catch and push prey into the nautilus' mouth.

eye

mouth

tentacle

Although the nautilus has a large eye, it does not have good eyesight. It uses smell and touch to find food in the dark.

Nautiluses have red-and-white spiral shells, which help to camouflage them.

Spot the difference

Which shell on this page is a nautilus?
Color the correct shell.

Piece by piece

Where do the missing parts of this nautilus go?

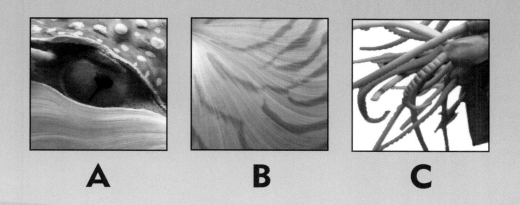

A   B   C

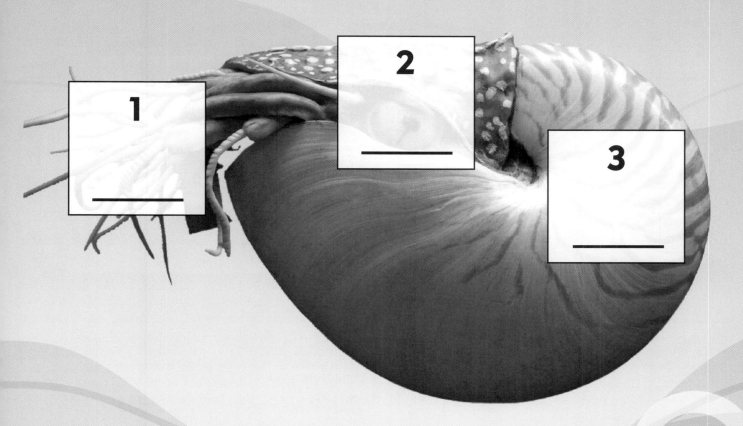

Cold oceans

The oceans are huge! They cover nearly two thirds of the Earth's surface. The oceans are deep, too. In some places they reach nearly 7 miles (11 kilometers) below the surface.

Most of the Earth's surface is covered by water.

Down in the ocean's depths, the water is very cold and dark. Nearer the surface, water is usually warmer because it is heated by sunlight. Most animals live at the surface.

African penguins hunt for fish in the cold waters of the Atlantic Ocean.

Animals of every shape and size live in salty ocean waters. The massive blue whale lives alongside tiny **microscopic** creatures called **plankton**. All ocean animals are suited to living in their watery world.

Tiny plankton need to be **magnified** for us to see them.

The ocean may be full of many more amazing animals, yet to be discovered.

The fantastic floating egg

Find out why eggs can float with this fun experiment!

You will need:
- 2 glasses
- 2 raw eggs in their shells
- 6 tablespoons of salt
- Tap water

WOW! The biggest ocean in the world is the Pacific Ocean.

1. Fill both glasses with tap water.

2. Add 6 tablespoons of salt to one of the glasses.

3. Put a raw egg in each glass.

4. Put a tick or a cross to say what happened to the eggs in the table below.

	floated	sank
Egg in tap water		
Egg in tap water with salt		

What happened?

Adding salt to water makes it heavier, or more dense. The tap water with salt is more dense than the egg, so it floats.

Orcas

The orca is also called the killer whale, even though it is actually a dolphin. It is one of the fastest ocean hunters. The orca's black-and-white markings make it easy to identify.

Orcas leap high out of the water, then plunge back into it. This is called breaching.

Some orcas stay in the same pod for their whole lives.

Orcas live in groups of about 30, called pods. Each pod has its own special language. Orcas "talk" to each other most of the time, so life in a pod can be very noisy!

Orcas will even swim onto the beach to catch a seal.

Orca art

Look at the small picture of the orca. Color in the larger orca below to match.

Pod puzzle

This orca has been separated from its pod. Help it follow the maze to find its friends.

Do you know many orcas normally live in a pod?

Humpback whales

The humpback whale is one of the giants of the ocean. This huge, heavy animal is also a strong swimmer, singer, and acrobat!

Whales give birth underwater. They push their young to the surface so they can breathe.

Humpback whales jump from the water and perform amazing leaps and twists in the air.

The humpbacks talk to each other by singing. Each whale has its own special song, made up of clicks and whistles.

Humpbacks open their mouth wide to take in lots of water. They eat tiny animals and plants, called plankton, that live in the water.

37

WARNiNG

How do whales stay warm?

Find out how *blubber* keeps whales warm!

You will need:

- 3 rubber gloves
- Petroleum jelly
- Large bowl
- Ice
- Water

WOW!

Humpback whales can weigh up to 45 tons!

1. Fill the bowl with cold water and ice.

2. Put the rubber gloves on both of your hands.

3. Ask an adult to help you cover one of the rubber gloves with petroleum jelly.

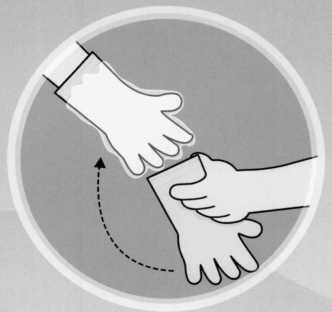

4. Put another rubber glove over the glove that has petroleum jelly on it.

5. Now put both hands in the cold water. Is one hand warmer?

What happened?

The petroleum jelly acted as blubber does on a whale. The two layers and jelly were thicker than one layer, so they kept that hand warmer.

Dolphins

Dolphins are intelligent and **acrobatic**. Their slim, sleek bodies slip easily through the water. These playful animals often leap out of the water or swim alongside boats.

Dolphins can leap high out of the water. They can also spin in the air and perform somersaults!

Dolphins have small, sharp teeth, which they use to eat fish.

Like killer whales, dolphins swim in groups called pods.

sound

Dolphins use sound to find food. They squeak and whistle. These sounds travel through the water and bump into other animals in the water. This creates echoes. The dolphin uses the echoes to work out where its prey is.

Swim with dolphins

These dolphins are playing in the ocean. Color in their fishy friends swimming below the water.

? Do you know which is the biggest species, or type, of dolphin?

Find the hidden treasure

There has been a shipwreck! Find the treasures in the word bank in the word search.

CROWN	DIAMOND	PAINTING
NECKLACE	BRACELET	COINS

D	G	B	R	M	X	Q	P
I	C	R	O	W	N	U	A
A	A	A	I	D	T	H	I
M	S	C	O	I	N	S	N
O	H	E	N	D	S	B	T
N	L	L	R	X	Z	N	I
D	T	E	B	W	A	L	N
P	P	T	P	D	N	I	G

Whale sharks

The whale shark is the largest fish in the ocean. Some grow as long as a bus and weigh a massive 16.5 tons.

The whale shark feeds by swimming along with its mouth wide open. It takes in huge mouthfuls of water, which it sieves through its gills. All the fish, squid, krill, and plankton in the water are eaten.

The whale shark's mouth is 4.5 feet (1.3 meters) wide, large enough to swallow a child!

Female whale sharks do not lay eggs. Instead, they give birth to as many as 300 baby sharks at one time.

The whale shark has a beautiful pattern of spots on its body.

Whale shark wonder

Fill in the missing word to complete the sentences below, using the word bank to help you.

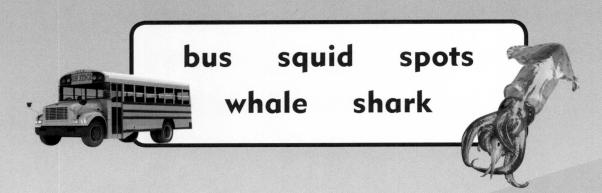

bus   squid   spots
whale   shark

A _____ _____

is the largest fish in the ocean.

A whale shark can be as big as a _____ .

A whale shark eats _____ .

A whale shark has _____

on its body.

Time for dinner!

Here are some of the things that whale sharks eat. Unscramble the word and then write it on the writing line.

rillk   k   _____

suidq   s   _____

lpnktona   p   _____

ishf   f   _____

Sunfish

The sunfish looks like a fish with half a body! Instead of a tail fin, its rounded body flattens at one end. Large fins at the top and bottom of its body help it to steer and stay upright.

The sunfish's large, round mouth is perfect for swallowing jellyfish. Unfortunately, many sunfish die after eating plastic bags, which look like jellyfish floating in the water.

The sunfish's mouth is always open and ready to catch its prey.

The sunfish is one of the largest fish in the ocean.

This massive fish can grow 14 feet (4 meters) tall—taller than two men. It weighs up to 4,400 pounds (2,000 kilograms)—about as heavy as 25 men!

Sunfish sometimes swim in groups of up to ten fish.

COUNT IT!

Sunfish sets

Count the sunfish in each set.
Write the answers in the boxes
next to the sets.

How many eggs can a female sunfish lay at one time?

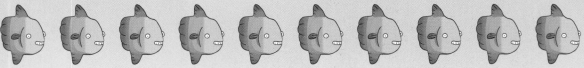

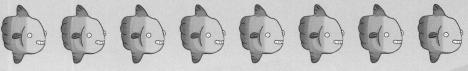

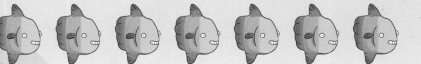

Find the answer on page 118

50

It all adds up

Circle the sunfish in each box. Write how many you find in the boxes below.

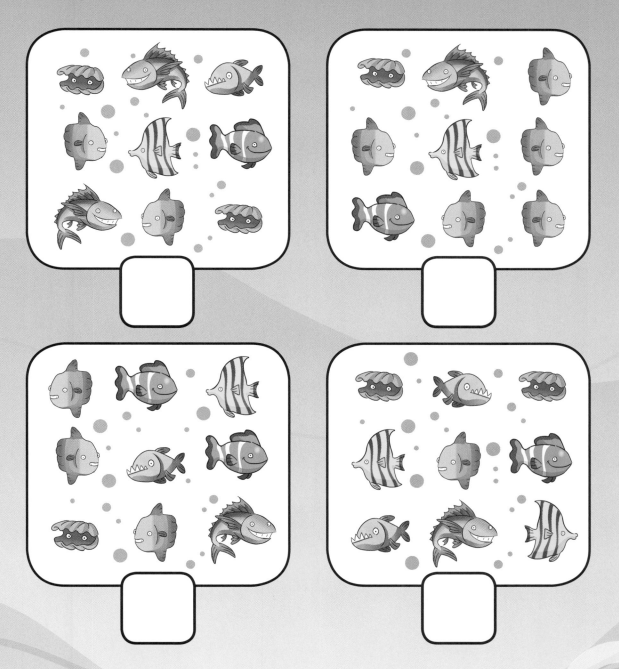

Jellyfish

The jellyfish is not a fish. It is an **invertebrate**—an animal without a backbone. The water supports the jellyfish's floppy body so it floats, carried around by the ocean's **currents**. If a jellyfish washes up onto a beach, it collapses into a soft blob.

A jellyfish's long tentacles trail behind its body.

A group of jellyfish is called a swarm.

Jellyfish live near the surface of the ocean.

The jellyfish's long, hanging tentacles are covered in tiny stings that explode with **poison** when touched. Some jellyfish stings are deadly to people.

Jellyfish fun!

Circle the words that describe parts of a jellyfish. Look at pages 52 and 53 for clues!

bones

tentacles

fins

stings

big mouths

tails

wings

Jellyfish jargon

Fill in the missing letter to complete the words that have to do with jellyfish. Use the letter bank to help you.

l   m   s   u   b

f___oats

swar___

poi___on

c___rrents

___lob

WOW!
There are more than 350 species of jellyfish.

Coral reefs

Coral reefs look like beautiful underwater gardens. They are the home of many colorful animals, including fish, anemones, starfish, and even sea snakes.

More than one million different types of animal live on coral reefs.

The Great Barrier Reef is made up of more than 900 islands.

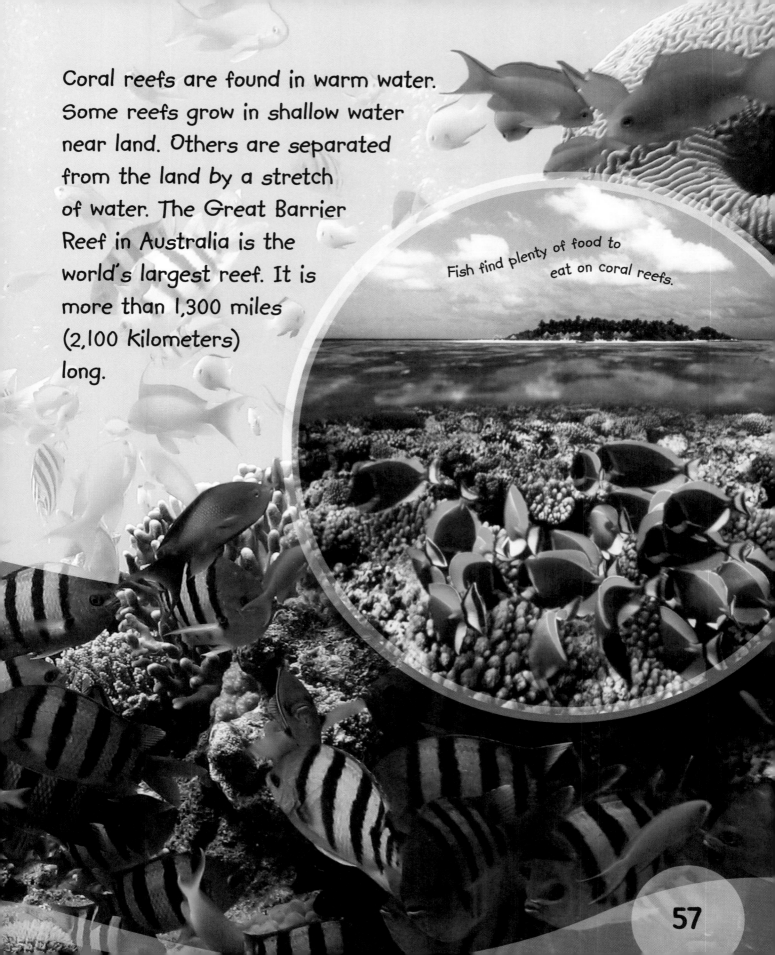

Coral reefs are found in warm water. Some reefs grow in shallow water near land. Others are separated from the land by a stretch of water. The Great Barrier Reef in Australia is the world's largest reef. It is more than 1,300 miles (2,100 kilometers) long.

Fish find plenty of food to eat on coral reefs.

Coral reef hide and seek

Lots of different kinds of fish live around coral reefs. Circle each kind of fish with a different colored crayon.

Now count the fish!

How many fish are there in all?

How many yellow fish are there?

How many yellow and blue fish are there?

How many black and white fish are there?

Corals

Coral reefs are built by groups of tiny animals called hard corals. The **corals** have stony **skeletons**. When a hard coral dies, another coral grows on top of its skeleton. Over hundreds of years, the bony skeletons knit together to form the reef.

When a coral reef forms a circle, it is called an **atoll**.

Corals come in many shapes and colors. Hard corals can look like bubbles or trumpets. Some soft corals look like fans and gently sway in the warm waters.

Hard coral looks a little like a brain!

Small creatures can easily hide in colorful fan coral.

Coral crazy!

Fill in the missing letters of these kinds of coral. Use the letter bank to help you.

? Do you know how long brain coral can live for?

n b i c

Fa ____ coral

Bub ____le coral

F____ nger coral

Lettu ____e coral

Find the answer on page 118

Coral word search

Using the work bank, find the
words in the search below.

CORAL   SWAY   REEF   ATOLL   SKELETON

A	S	C	S	W	A	Y
Q	S	T	K	M	L	P
F	E	R	E	E	F	M
A	T	O	L	L	G	H
N	J	P	E	F	G	J
J	L	Q	T	X	Z	Y
F	T	C	O	R	A	L
A	L	B	N	W	L	O

Lionfish

Darting around the reef is the lionfish. It has a striking, stripy body. This fish may look beautiful, but the spines on its **fins** give a painful sting.

Lionfish sometimes hunt together in groups to catch their **prey**.

The lionfish's stripes warn predators to stay away.

Lionfish only use their stings for defense. If another animal threatens it, the lionfish does not need to swim away. It can simply point its deadly **spines** toward the enemy.

Lionfish spread out their fins to catch prey.

Lionfish are hunters. They corner prey with their large fins before swallowing them in one gulp.

COLOR CRAZY!

Reef life

These lionfish live around a coral reef. Draw the coral and color the seaweed to complete the reef.

? Do you know what kind of food lionfish eat?

Find the answer on page 118

Color by numbers

Follow the numbers to color
in the lionfish.

1. Brown
2. Orange
3. Gray
4. Blue
5. Black

67

Clown fish

Sea anemones are animals that live on the reef. They have stinging tentacles that protect them from **predators**.

Most fish stay well away from sea anemones, but not the clown fish. The anemone's sting does not harm this brightly colored fish, so it makes its home between the anemone's tentacles.

Clown fish are covered in a layer of slime to protect them from the anemone's sting.

Whole families of clown fish can live in one anemone.

The clown fish also gets its food from the anemone. It eats the anemone's leftovers, such as shrimp. In return, the clown fish cleans the anemone's tentacles and scares away other fish.

COUNT IT!

Clowning around with clown fish

Spot the clown fish that is the odd one out. Circle it, then write how many pairs of fish you can see in the box below.

How many pairs? ☐

Counting

Count the clown fish in the anemones and write down how many you can see in each.

? What was the name of the clown fish in "Finding Nemo?"

Find the answer on page 118

Reef sharks

With its wide jaws and jagged teeth, the reef shark is a fierce hunter. Most sharks have a slim body and a powerful tail fin, perfect for gliding through water.

Octopuses, crabs, and sea snakes are just some of the animals hunted by reef sharks.

Reef sharks have rows of deadly, jagged teeth.

Large flaps of skin make it difficult to spot the wobbegong shark on the seabed.

Sharks, such as the large black-tip reef shark and the small wobbegong shark, swim up and down the reef, on the lookout for fish and squid. They often hide in caves during the day and come out at night to hunt.

SPOT THE DIFFERENCE

Reef sharks

Where do the missing parts of this reef shark go?

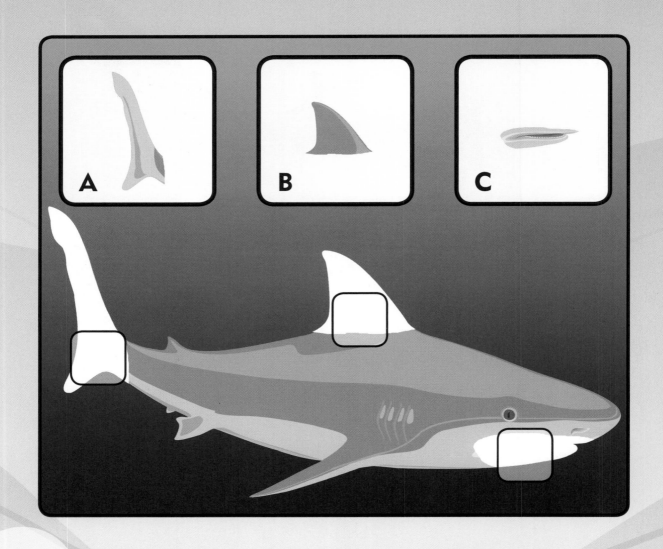

What doesn't belong?

Sometimes, people throw garbage into the ocean that can harm the coral reef. Circle five things that don't belong on the reef, using the word bank to help you.

**soda can   shoe   bottle
oil drum   umbrella**

Find the answer on page 118

Do you know how many teeth a reef shark has?

75

Green turtles

The sea turtle is an odd-looking animal. It has scaly skin and most of its body is covered by a tough shell. It has a large, beaklike mouth that it uses to graze on sea plants. The sea turtle is a reptile.

The female green turtle digs a hole in the sand and lays her eggs in it.

Green turtles are often seen swimming in shallow water near the coast.

The newly hatched sea turtle makes its way to the sea.

Each year, female sea turtles return to the beach where they were born to lay their own eggs. About two months later, the eggs hatch. The tiny turtles dig their way out of the sand and dash to the water.

ALPHABET JUMBLE

Turtle race

Help the turtles make it to the water by tracing a path that follows the letters in alphabetical order. Start with the A and end with the Z.

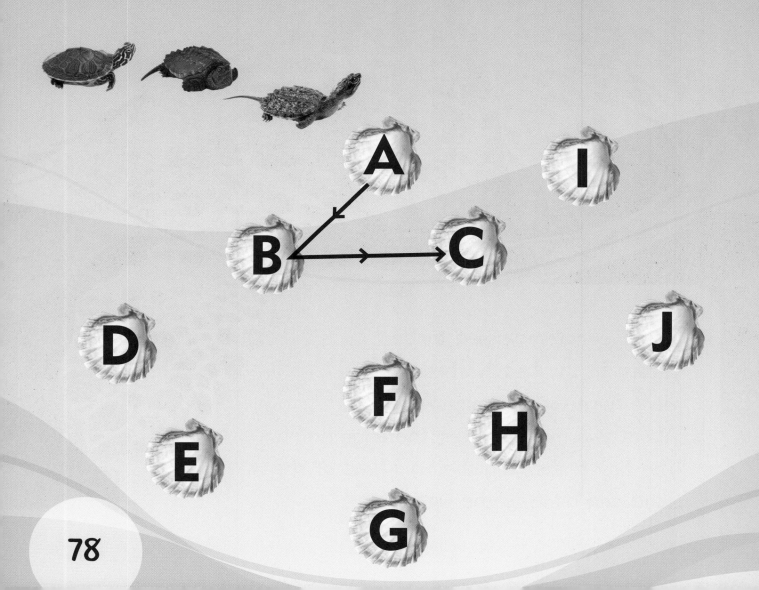

78

Giant clams

Two huge shells protect
the giant clam's soft body.
It cannot move, so stays in
the same spot on the reef.

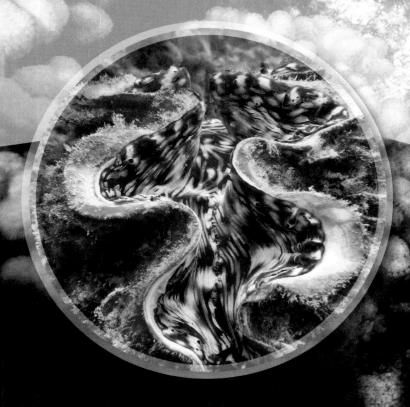

If a clam senses danger,
it quickly closes its shells.

To eat, the clam sucks in food through special tubes. It also gets food from tiny plants called zooxanthellae that live inside its body.

The oldest clams weigh about 660 pounds (300 kilograms) —that is as heavy as four men!

The giant clam's bright colors come from the tiny plants that live inside it.

Clam crazy!

Draw a line to match the giant clams that are exactly alike.

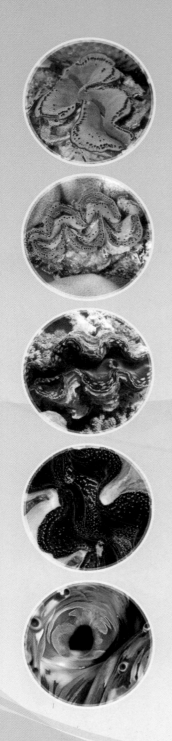

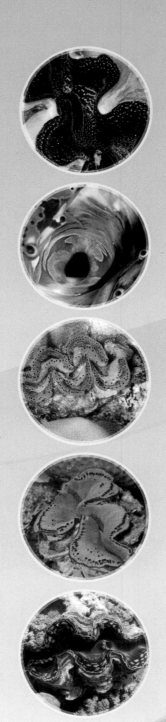

Color by numbers

Follow the numbers to create your own giant clam, then color it in.

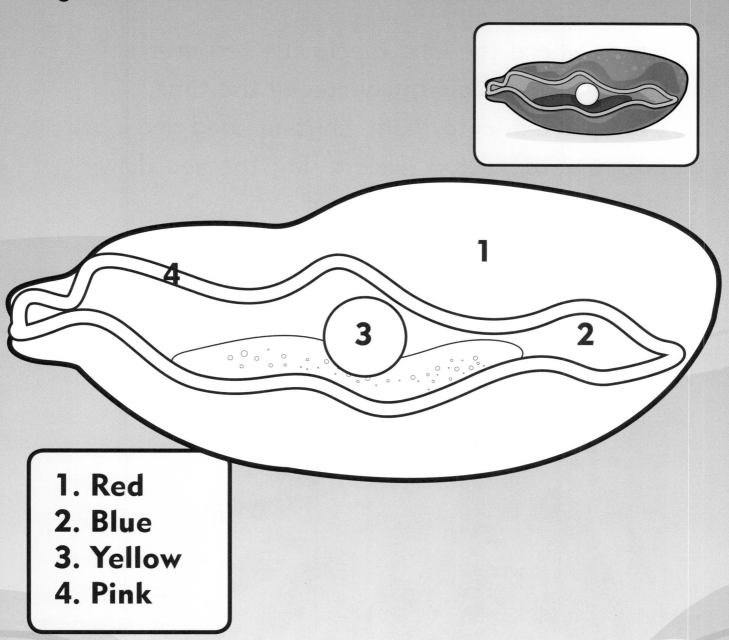

1. Red
2. Blue
3. Yellow
4. Pink

Shallow-water homes

Areas where the land meets the sea are called coasts. Coasts change all the time. Waves crash onto them, shifting sand and breaking up rocks. Twice a day, the sea flows up to the **beach** and then falls away. These movements of the sea are called tides.

Kelp forests are found in coastal waters. They are homes to the animals that live there.

Animals, such as sharks and seals, live in the coast's shallow waters. Hermit crabs and starfish live on the seabed. Along the coast, there are also thick forests of green kelp, or seaweed, which provide homes for fish and other animals.

Many fish live in the shallow water along coasts.

Waves rise and fall over rocky coasts.

WATER WORLD

You will need:

- 1 clear plastic bottle with a top
- 1 tablespoon of cooking oil
- 2 cups of water
- Blue food coloring

Make your own ocean

Get ready to make some waves with this fun experiment!

1. Fill the bottle with 2 cups of water.

2. Add 8–10 drops of blue food coloring.

3. Add the cooking oil.

4. Put the lid on and shake the water.

5. Tilt the bottle back and forth to make some waves!

WOW!
In most coastal areas, the tides come in and out twice a day.

What happened?

The water and oil do not mix together. The oil stays on top of the water, and moves in the way that a wave does across the surface.

Hermit crabs

Most crabs are protected by a hard shell, but the hermit crab has to borrow one from another animal. Instead of growing its own shell, the hermit crab pushes its soft body into an empty shell left by a sea snail.

Small animals called sea anemones attach themselves to the hermit crab's shell. They feed on the crab's leftover meals.

sea anemone

hermit crab

When the hermit crab grows bigger, it finds another empty shell that fits. It pulls its body out of the old shell and moves into a new one.

This hermit crab is looking for the perfect shell.

Hermit crabs have ten legs and two large eyes.

Hermit crab mania!

Draw a line to connect the shell to the hermit crab below.

Next crab in line

Complete the hermit crab pattern! Color the crabs in the right order.

Limpets

A limpet is a snail that lives on rocky shores and in kelp forests. It has a cone-shaped shell that looks like a pointed hat.

The limpet moves around using its large foot.

foot

The limpet creeps over rocks in search of tiny plants called **algae** to eat. When the tide goes out, it returns to its favorite spot on the rock. It uses its strong muscular foot to cling onto the rock. It does not move until the tide comes in again.

Limpets can survive out of water for many hours if they are fixed to a rock.

SPOT IT!

Look out for the limpets!

Circle the 10 limpets hidden on this rock.

WOW!
A limpet is a kind of fresh and saltwater snail!

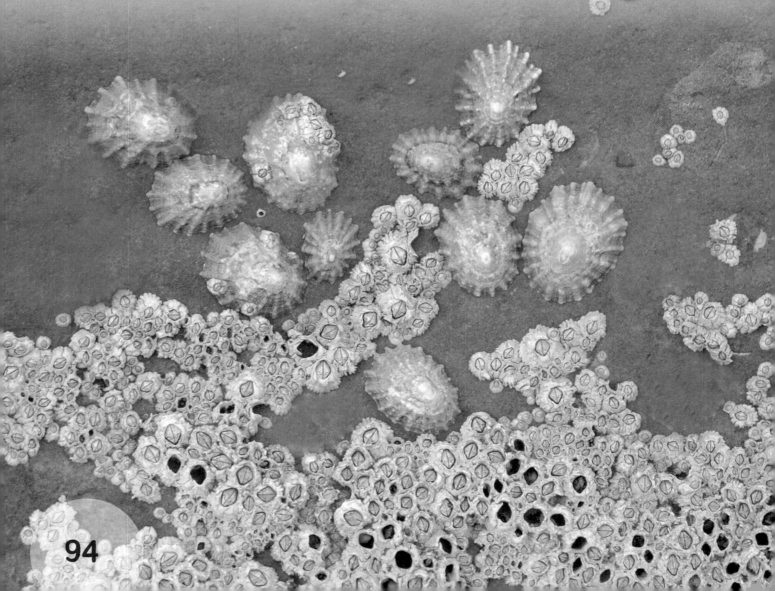

Spot the difference

Circle the shell that belongs to a limpet.

Starfish

The starfish is an invertebrate. An invertebrate is an animal that does not have a backbone. The starfish has at least five arms. Underneath the arms are tubelike feet with suckers. It uses the suckers to grip prey, such as **mussels**.

The starfish can use its strong feet to move pebbles.

Starfish pour the contents of their stomach over their prey to turn it into a mushy liquid. The starfish then sucks up the liquid.

Starfish can move at a speed of more than 3 feet (1 meter) a minute.

If a predator pulls off one of the starfish's arms, the arm will grow back.

An arm-y of starfish

Starfish sometimes have more than five arms. Count how many arms each starfish has, then write the answers in the boxes.

All about arms

Add up the number of starfish.
Write the answer in the box.

Find the answer on page 118

Octopuses

The octopus is an eight-armed animal. Each arm is covered with suckers that grip prey. The octopus uses its powerful **beak** to rip up and crush the prey into small pieces.

The octopus has two rows of suckers on each arm.

When an octopus is threatened, it releases a cloud of black ink into the water. This confuses the predator, so the octopus can slip away.

An octopus moves by crawling along the seabed using its arms. It can also swim very fast by pushing a jet of water out of its body at high speed.

The octopus' long arms are called tentacles.

The octopus squirts black ink from a tube inside its body

Spot the difference

Circle five differences between these two pictures of an octopus.

Lots of legs!

Finish this picture of an octopus by coloring in its eight legs.

WOW!
Most species of octopus have three hearts.

Eagle rays

The eagle ray has a pointed nose and a flattened body with huge winglike fins. It swims slowly through the water by flapping its wings. Occasionally, it leaps out of the water.

The mouth of the eagle ray is on the underside of its body.

Spotted eagle rays often swim in shallow water along sandy coasts.

mouth

Eagle rays search for food on the seabed.

The ray uses its strong teeth to crush the shells of seabed creatures, such as crabs and mussels. Its long tail ends in **poisonous spines**, which the ray uses to defend itself from attackers.

Eagle ray writing

Trace these words to do with eagle rays.
Try writing them yourself on the lines below.

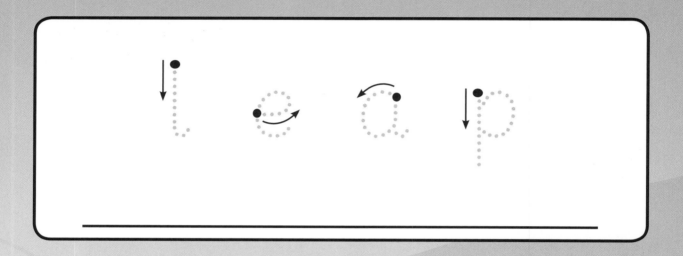

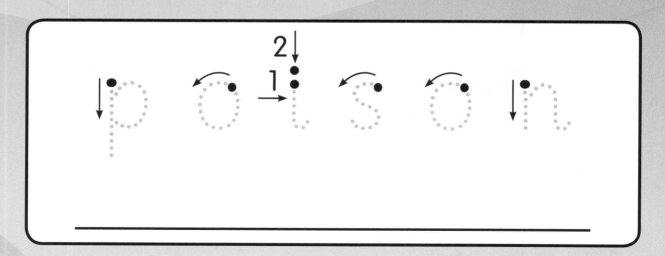

Eagle ray match-up

Label the different parts of the eagle ray on the writing lines. Use the word bank to help you.

? Do you know where the eggs of eagle rays hatch?

fin   eye   tail
mouth   teeth

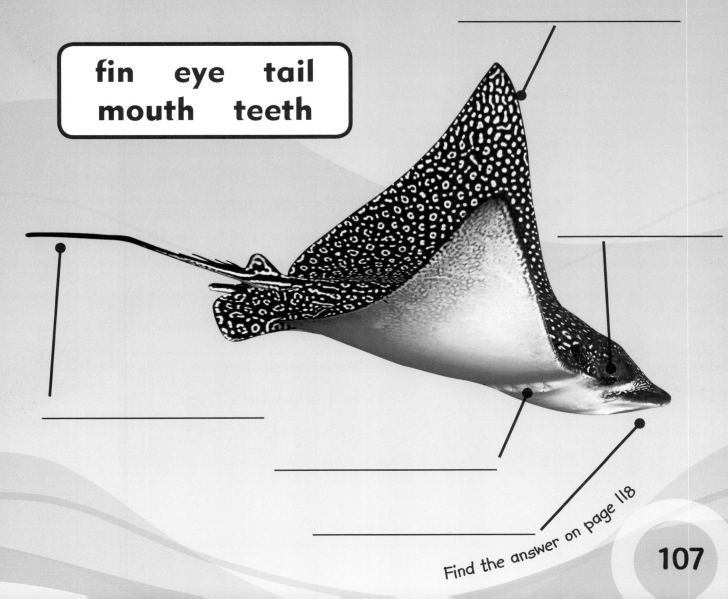

Find the answer on page 118

Seals

Seals are **mammals**, but instead of legs, they have **flippers**. Their sleek, streamlined bodies make them expert swimmers.

Seals are clumsy on land, but very graceful in the water.

Like other mammals, seals have **lungs**, so they must come to the surface to breathe. However, seals can hold their breath for nearly an hour when they swim underwater.

Seals slowly wriggle onto land using their front flippers.

Seals use their front flippers to steady themselves when they are swimming slowly.

Who is swimming with the seal?

Color in the fish that are swimming around the ocean.

I see the seal

Label the different body parts of this seal. Use the word bank to help you.

flippers   fur
nose   eye   whiskers

Seahorses

The seahorse does not look like a fish. Its body is covered in armor-like scales and it uses its long tail to wrap itself around pieces of seaweed.

Some seahorses are disguised to look like bits of coral or seaweed.

Seahorses wrap their tail around seaweed so they are not carried away by the current.

The seahorse swims upright in the water using tiny fan-shaped fins.

fin

The female seahorse passes her eggs to the male. He puts them in a pouch on the front of his body. He cares for the eggs for several weeks until the young seahorses are ready to live on their own.

Seahorse search

Find the terms in the word bank in the word search below.

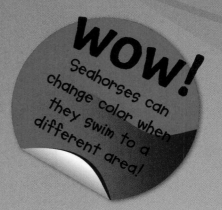

WOW!
Seahorses can change color when they swim to a different area!

| SEAHORSE | SEAWEED |
| EGGS | FINS | SCALES |

N	S	F	I	N	S	Y	S
O	S	T	K	M	L	P	S
S	E	A	H	O	R	S	E
A	S	C	A	L	E	S	A
N	J	E	P	F	G	J	W
J	L	G	T	X	Z	Y	E
O	T	G	E	W	A	L	E
M	P	S	Y	W	Y	O	D

Mixed-up seahorses

Unscramble the words that have to do with seahorses. Write them on the lines below.

ouchp

_____

sclesa

_____

ailt

_____

sfin

_____

weedsea

_____

115

Glossary

Acrobatic
Able to twist, turn, and jump easily.

Algae
Tiny plants that are often eaten by sea animals.

Beach
An area of sand where the sea meets the land.

Beak
The hard snout used to catch prey.

Coral
An animal from which coral reefs are built.

Coral reef
A group of hard rocks made of coral.

Current
The flow of water.

Echo
The noise made when sound bounces off objects.

Environment
The area in which an animal or plant lives.

Fin
The part of a fish used to swim and steer.

Flipper
A broad, flat limb of a mammal that lives in water.

Gill
An opening in its body through which an underwater animal breathes.

Invertebrate
An animal without a backbone.

Lungs
The part of the body that
an animal uses to breathe.

Magnify
Make something look
bigger than it really is.

Mammal
An animal that is covered with hair
and gives birth to live young.

Microscopic
Too tiny to see without an
instrument called a microscope.

Muscular
Having strong muscles.

Mussel
Sea creature with a soft
body and hard shell.

Plankton
Small plants and animals that
float in the surface waters of
the oceans.

Poison
Something that can harm
or even kill.

Poisonous spines
Sharp parts of an animal's body
that can hurt or kill another animal
if touched.

Predator
An animal that hunts
other animals.

Prey
An animal that is hunted
by other animals.

Reptile
An animal with scaly skin that
lays eggs.

Shrimp
A small sea creature with
a shell around its body.

Skeleton
The framework of bones supporting the body.

Spine
A long, sharp point.

Streamlined
Having a smooth shape that moves easily through water.

Submersible
Vehicle used to explore underwater.

Tentacle
A limb of a sea creature. It is used for holding, and sometimes for stinging.

Answers

p.35   There can be more than 30 orcas living in a pod.

p.38   There are 32 different species of dolphin.

p.50   A female sunfish can make more than 300 million eggs at one time.

p.62   Brain coral can live for up to 900 years.

p.66   Lionfish eat shellfish such as shrimp and crabs.

p.71   The clown fish in "Finding Nemo" was called Nemo.

p.75   Reef sharks can have up to 3,000 teeth.

p.99   Starfish have eyes on the ends of their arms.

p.107   Some species of eagle rays' eggs hatch inside the mother's body.

Index

Index